Are you ready to Love Yourself a Black Man?

Kris Godspeed Amos

Are you ready to Love Yourself a Black Man?

Kris Godspeed Amos

Are You Ready to Love Yourself a Black Man?
Copyright©2019 Kris Godspeed Amos
All Rights Reserved
Published by Unsolicited Press
Printed in the United States of America.
First Edition 2019.

All rights reserved. Printed in the United States of America. No part of this book may be used or reproduced in any manner whatsoever without written permission except in the case of brief quotations embodied in critical articles or reviews.

Attention schools and businesses: for discounted copies on large orders, please contact the publisher directly. Books are brought to the trade by Ingram.

For information contact:
Unsolicited Press
Portland, Oregon
www.unsolicitedpress.com
orders@unsolicitedpress.com
619-354-8005

Cover Design: Kathryn Gerhardt
Editor: S.R. Stewart
ISBN: 978-1-950730-06-3

Contents

Are you ready to love yourself a Black Man?	6
Black Deficiency	9
Yearbook Awards	9
Masculinity So Fragile	10
Synthesis	12
Nothing Else Matters	14
Black Card Revoked	16
To Be Heard	17
Restrained	19
The Scar of Doubt	20
The Ex	22
Mechanism of Injury	23
F33.2	24
Break-Up	25
Afraid of the Dark	27
Dr. Malcolm Luther King X	29

Are you ready to love yourself a Black Man?

Before continuing to engage in your relationship
ask yourself,

Are you ready to love you a black man?

As beautifully un-appealing
as it seems,
you may not be prepared for what may come of it.

When you enter this relationship,
there may be unexpected consequences
that come from it.

Be prepared to
endure the struggle that comes with it;

The stereotypes linked to the sequences of our genes.
We're seen as property
valued at generational profits;
Our physiques celebrated,
our minds demeaned.

People are willing to bear our seeds with the goal
of flushing our contributions through filtered
American dreams.

Centuries-old ownership systems corrupted our psyche.
We're at war with ourselves,
preparing to battle evil

as it leads us in the name of God Almighty.

The lust of our appearance intoxicates and entices,
and seduces you into the struggle of intracultural vices.

You sure you want to love yourself a black man?

With the possession of talent that surpasses science,
we conquer fear like an inquisitive toddler.

Undesirable traits leave us vulnerable
to neglectful fathers,
So why bother?

Mom?
Dad?

Are you ready to love a black man?

How could they?
Why would they?

Only expected to survive a quarter of the life
expectancy, why waste the time?
Deceptive stimuli influences and distracts the most
magnificent of minds,
There's no wonder why puppets who vote
for independence get hung by their own vines.

We were programmed to not love ourselves,
So why would anyone else?
Impaled with distorted perceptions of self-love,
sexuality, and mental health,

We're portrayed as molds of desire used to straddle
whenever someone has a need to be quelled.

The sky has never been a limit.
How can we constrict ourselves
when the universe is expanding in our image?

We leap gates, barriers, and fences
to score for someone else's business.
But when shadows are cast to restrict us to our limits,
Coach...

Are you willing to love yourself a nigga?

America doesn't allow us to experience what love means.
Our peers, family, and children contribute to the
       schemes.
They don't love us.
They love the idea of being able to *control* what we
think.

Given the provided,
the question stands,

Are you sure
you're ready to love yourself a black man?

Black Deficiency

Many decades prior,
I would have been considered property of a white man.

Hardly considered human,
No thought given to my life's potential
if given the right chance.

Why travel to the past and consider the 'what if's'?
We're free, right?

No one lynched or fire-hosed— if life were the past,
I wouldn't have the intellectual capacity
to communicate and would be hesitant
because of the risks.

When racism is claimed,
That's typically the image some think of.

But,
I'm not stupid,
I know you're not either,
So I'm not convinced of any denial you speak of.

You get so offended
whenever someone pulls the
"race card".

As if the wound is too brutal to endure.
I get it—I can even see your fake scars,

It makes sense it took you longer to mature.

I was born into a generational entrapment
from the effects of racism through epigenetics.
Predisposed to impoverished conditions
based on trauma already embedded.

21st-century prejudice
and discrimination,
objective:
deny it.

King of the jungle my ass,
supremacy doesn't even exist in the savanna for lions.

I view America with indifference.
Are you willing to expand your perspectives,
be more empathetic,
and listen?

Or will you continue to be implicit
        in your reinforcement of a supremacist system?

Yearbook Awards

Society roams the hallway
by the lockers
where the cool kids rule.

High school never left us.

A testament of progress to how our species
        developed,
The theories of evolution
do not apply to our social connections.

Morals are projected to others through detoxification.
If behavior isn't conducted in a manner
conducive to our expectations,
Then we sacrifice your wellness
for the betterment of entertainment.
Despite multiple opportunities,
we rebuke suggestions of changing.
-"Most entitled",
and the award goes to…
America's culture of behaving.

Masculinity So Fragile

We take advantage of nature's most valued creation.
The woman.
Succumbing to our savage impatience,
we make her a victim to our rabid temptations.

No apologies given.
No apologies taken.

From being appreciated for our
        creation,
To being treated as the recycling bins of our nation.

The world owes her the rightful place at the throne.
Masculinity so fragile,
It needs to be packaged alone,
And handled with care,
Otherwise,
it would crack on its own.

We take her for granted.
Lying,
Cheating,
Using, and abusing,
and yet she still manages
to support us
despite our habits.
Why are belittling names used to identify her social
        status?
Our lives wouldn't exist
if she weren't here to have them.

We're responsible for the damages,
and the costs of fixing them.

Our failure to communicate
leads to arguments of who's the biggest victim.
Behavior that's an infection to the safety of women,
We haven't found a cure for our insolence.

Synthesis

Forgive me for the damage I've inflicted.
I offer my vices and sacrifice
my desires as a testament to how much I'm
committed. 👰‍♂️.
Looking to add meaning to my existence
and I'm wondering if you're willing
to provide assistance?

You've become the gravity to my soul,
You keep my mind and body from detaching 🫂.
Aided in my battles without thought
to any consequences that could happen.
Never needed assistance in the past,
But I'm quite fond of this attachment.
Memories of you loiter in my synapses
until I run out of resources,
short circuit,
and collapse.

I was hopeless to the existential sensation.
Playing Russian Roulette with creation,
I hit a bullseye while at the gun range. 😇.

Our wavelengths intersect for the creation of a new
spectrum.
Part of the journey involves discovering unsolved
      equations,

and pushing boundaries of what is described as destined.
We added a variable to the formula,
allowing us to solve the initial question 👫.
Now we orbit the courtyards of Eden,
and our actions finally led to a moment of conception 👶.

Nothing Else Matters

I separate insignificant pleasures and volatile desires
       to be with you.
Many people sacrifice themselves
to provide better circumstances
for their seeds to improve,
and in this case with me
it would still be true,
but at the same time

unfair to you.

You look to me for guidance and growth.
If I remain stagnant in my future hopes
by focusing on your goals,
Who are you going to look up to
when you need to pass the threshold of us both?

My peak is for you.
When I was 19 years old
with no facial hair,
and developing in my youth,
I was still thinking of you.
You can ask around if you don't believe that it's true.
I was shedding tears because you weren't born yet,
too eager and desperate to meet up with you.

I wasn't ready.
So I abled myself for your arrival.
Accomplishing milestones,
dispositioning the earth to find you.
Evidence suggested I was not prepared

to bring you into this world,
> but I still tried to.

And now,
after years of preparation
I'm honored to be chosen as the father
you've been assigned to.

Black Card Revoked

I have a biracial baby.

So, what?
Why have a problem with it?

I took the risk of losing my status
in the cultural paradigm
because I have a daughter whose skin is different?

I'm done apologizing for people's ignorance.

Since I didn't use racial prejudice
to guide my love interests,

I'm now a part of the problems
connected to the black image.

To Be Heard

Who cares about a man in love?
The idea is tucked neatly under the waist of
    "get the hell out of here".

You don't want to hear
how I process my happiness, heartbreak, or joy.
The value of relationships was lost after the split of
    Boyz II Men.
So during the transition from
    boys to men,
The harmonies bound by love
were stripped therein.

My tears are worth the value
of a penny in the 23rd century.
Resources depleted,
I'm no longer able to afford the costs of empathy.
It's a luxury not discounted
for those who struggle with compensation.
Can I offer you a dollar for *my* thoughts?
Times are hard these days,
a penny was a miscalculation.

Listen to me complain like a
"punk",
"wimp",
or other suggestive terms
that describe my "weakened state."

Love is genderless,

Pure,
Divine,

and independent of time,
It metabolizes emotions to be in sync with fate.

Sound travels through the air at approximately three hundred and forty-five meters per second.

My emotions speak outside the range of acceptable
    social perspectives.

"Dogs are a man's best friend",
    was more than a coincidental suggestion.

To be heard,
I had to develop conversion methods
so the message
could reach the listener's mind for nonbiased inspection.

No matter the modified properties of the universe,
listeners of this generation
would still reject the expression.

"Return to sender";
    Just as I expected.

Restrained

I don't know who I am,
or maybe it's you trying to change me.
I conform to your needs
realizing I'm not the same me.

You don't notice the difference.
It's beginning to make me angry.

Forced,
Coerced,
and placed in a controlled environment
where attempts to defend my sanity
is blocked by security.

Let me compensate you for being victimized.
You have a biased cast
acting the roles you scripted,
I give you props' and you use them to improvise.

I made myself look crazy saving face for you.
I assume you turn about
whenever you must face the truth.
I opened myself,
packed other rooms,
evicted past tenants
and made space for you.
Agreed to terms,
until you voided your own contract
conveniently erasing the proof.

Your indecency blinded you
from acquiring a new sense of self-awareness.
I worked on treating your symptoms
until I induced my own impairment.

We were once on the same page,
The same sentence,
The same word;

We were the ink.

Then we parted paragraphs,
Sheets,
And now we're no longer in the same genre,
Two different books
incomplete.

You can't cut yourself and sue the blacksmith for
        damages.
Your self-inflicted wounds bled through all of my
        bandages.

Although causalities were provided to both parties,
You left with the advantage.
I'm determined to be at fault
without being given the opportunity to challenge it.

The Scar of Doubt

Dirty clothes never heal.
Stains become resistant to bleach
regardless of how they feel.

Evolution stitches into fabric.
Expensive outfits that begin to trend
fall in value when they are on the clearance rack
not matching what the current fad is.

You lose confidence when you wear
the same thing on a consistent basis.

Holes in denim,
Always falling from over worn laces.

New outfits are already out of style.
Returns are denied,
Because the fine print indicates
all purchases are final.

Never enough to wash a load.
Envious of fashion models,
Can you spare your detergent for a cycle of clean
        clothes?

The Ex

I get ahead of myself,
I trust despite better judgment.
My vulnerabilities are on display
seeking the attention of a loved one.

Failure is not sacred.
Why express gratitude when unsuccessful?
Attempts to attract humility were futile,
Modest qualities are unimpressive.

I'm sorry for any trouble
I've caused to anyone
I've interacted with.

I want to reciprocate positive energy
with anyone that can be impacted.

I know I can't be that bad of a person,
is this all the pain from my past actions?

I thought I awoke from my depressive state,

Close my eyes and it's back again.

Mechanism of Injury

My future was rewritten.
It was ciphered in my chromosomes
to remain peacefully hidden.
Designed to function with one condition,
Redirect any stimuli that can place it in a threatening
        position;

But it didn't.

Piece by piece,
Ligaments are reattached
to become one again.
Fear follows the neuropathy
of innervating my impulses,
so I can be ready to run again.

Every time I restructure myself, I get broken and
        separated.
I don't know if I will make it.
Ashamed.
Vulnerable.
Naked.

I'm exposed to all.
This is reportedly normal,
we are all supposed to fall.
Before taking the first steps,
You must learn to crawl,
And think outside of the box,
but what if your skull is inflamed and scarred?

F33.2

I am the clinical definition of depression.

My symptoms are not worthy.
Visitors appear without warning
or indication they will be arriving early.

I see you,
You are overheard,
and have exhausted your welcome.

Don't go.

I need you like everything else
in my life that's unhelpful.

At least you're here.
I feel you,
But hate you because of it.
After finalizing my happiness,
I can look you in the face and say I'm down with
        this.

Here I am stuck again.

No matter how many times I get motivated enough to
        announce,
"Fuxk this shit!",

As soon as I reach a peaceful state of being,
        Here you come again.

Break Up

I've never been happy.
Despite many strides,
I ask for an early death.
Been suicidal for two decades,
if I weren't hopeful for a successful future,
I would have surely left.

What purpose do I provide this world?

As an entity for people to extract love from?
To absorb the suffering of others
and take on more problems for me to run from?

I never thought I belonged.

Interacting with my peers,
I never felt welcomed.
Few made me feel loved and appreciated,
which were feelings I experienced very seldom.

I saw death approaching,
It turned the other way.
I initiated the pursuit,
and now we're in a chase.

Soon it will return,
and my request will be granted.
Will I regret the reality,
and plead I only panicked?

Will people see me as a coward?
Someone who lacked the strength to survive?
Come to conclusions on what I should have
done,
changed,
or tried?

Will they feel responsible?
Take it personally that I died?
Feel regret about our interactions when I was alive?

No faults can be exchanged,
the only shame should be mine.

I can't take my own advice,

"How are you feeling?"
My response:
"I'm fine".

Is this another phase?
I know I've said this several times.
I can't take away the pain,
and I apologize for the crying.

It's not you,
It's me.

Afraid of the Dark

I write poetry I don't understand.
Do I have the credentials to call myself a poet?
Entered into this genre where I do not belong,
The color of my ink is erased and goes unnoticed.

I have blank documents for sale.
Empty sheets of paper.
Undocumented keystrokes.
Dye colonized from nature.

My microphone was taken from me.
My platform,
My stage,
My audience,
My poetry.

I was migrated to the beach
but my heart caused it to snow.
It orbits a planet far from the sun,
never escaping the sensations of the cold.

Medication in my grave,
I do not rest in peace.
My memories became zombies,
They lurk for positive thoughts to eat.

My voice is immobilized,
space has restricted its movement.

I live with pain as an
        alarm clock.
I go every day trying to
        snooze it.

My trauma is traumatized.
Hope was last seen entering the event horizon.

Demons travel from the corners of the universe,
breaking dimensional planes
to recruit me to the other life.

Don't be afraid of the dark.

Dr. Malcolm Luther King X

I'm glad I'm distinguished enough
to be recognized as a threat to you.

I evoke
envy,
anger,
and insecurity
simply by sitting next to you.

I can appreciate why.
You let your fears get the best of you.

Let me stress this to you,

We are passed the stages of protest.
You claim to have our best interests,
but are more pressed
on pushing false perceptions of morality
to enforce more stress.

White flags are never seen waving
in our neighborhood.
Messages from here do not get
interpreted correctly.
Reaching for an item can cause one to fear for his life.
This isn't the generation
that's going to continue to turn the left cheek.

Wrongful deaths are justified

by those able to articulate unpunishable crimes.
Pressure may be the only mechanism
capable of releasing the tension
        this time.
Linguistics isn't enough to convince us
        this time,
We're using conviction
        this time.
Charges brought against oppression gets dismissed
        each time.

Sounds waves don't travel through the space
of the unfortunate.
You are only heard speaking
if you're able to afford it.

It was never apples and oranges.
The *apple* wasn't supposed to be eaten.

Instead of being classified together as fruit,
We're left to rot,
labeled as unappealing.

We are an endangered species,
they want us to continue losing our lives.
It's past due to evict the oppressors,
and I plan to move in tonight.
Every time we murder each other,
we are only proving them right.

And if this doesn't get me killed…

Then I must not have been doing it right.

Are You Sure You're Willing to Love Yourself a Black Man?

About the Press

Unsolicited Press is a small press in Portland, Oregon. The team produces award-winning poetry, fiction, and creative nonfiction.

Learn more at www.unsolicitedpress.com